RACHEL CARSON

Essential Lives

RACHEL CARSON

PIONEER OF ENVIRONMENTALISM

by Scott Gillam

Content Consultant:
Peter Bower, PhD, Senior Lecturer, Department of
Environmental Science, Barnard College/Columbia University

ABDO
Publishing Company

CREDITS

Published by ABDO Publishing Company, 8000 West 78th Street, Edina, Minnesota 55439. Copyright © 2011 by Abdo Consulting Group, Inc. International copyrights reserved in all countries. No part of this book may be reproduced in any form without written permission from the publisher. The Essential Library™ is a trademark and logo of ABDO Publishing Company.

Printed in the United States of America,
North Mankato, Minnesota
052010
092010

 THIS BOOK CONTAINS AT LEAST 10% RECYCLED MATERIALS.

Editor: Holly Saari
Copy Editor: Paula Lewis
Interior Design and Production: Becky Daum
Cover Design: Becky Daum

Library of Congress Cataloging-in-Publication Data
Gillam, Scott.
  Rachel Carson : pioneer of environmentalism / Scott Gillam.
      p. cm. — (Essential lives)
  Includes bibliographical references and index.
  ISBN 978-1-61613-511-9
  1. Carson, Rachel, 1907-1964—Juvenile literature. 2.
Biologists—United States—Biography—Juvenile literature. 3.
Environmentalists—United States—Biography—Juvenile literature.
I. Title.
  QH31.C33G66 2010
  333.95′16092—dc22
                            2010000539

TABLE OF CONTENTS

*In 1952, a farming town was fogged with
the pesticide DDT to kill mosquitoes.*

SOUNDING THE ALARM

The opening lines of *Silent Spring* may sound
like the beginning of a science fiction
novel, but they describe true events:

> There was once a town in the heart of America where all life
> seemed to live in harmony with its surroundings. The town lay

in the midst of a checkerboard of prosperous farms, with fields of grain and hillsides of orchards. . . . Then a strange blight crept over the area and everything began to change. Some evil spell had settled on the community: mysterious maladies swept the flocks of chickens; the cattle and sheep sickened and died. . . . The farmers spoke of much illness among their families. . . . There had been several sudden and unexplained deaths.[1]

Though the first chapter is titled "A Fable for Tomorrow," its author, Rachel Carson, explained that each incident had occurred. She also stated that the incidents could become worse if the public did not determine the causes and prevent them from continuing. Carson, a former marine biologist with the U.S. Fish and Wildlife Service, carefully examined evidence surrounding these situations. She concluded that dichlorodiphenyltrichloroethane, known as DDT, and other chemical pesticides caused the illness and deaths she described.

A Balancing Act

In 1963, CBS televised a documentary about Rachel Carson. Robert White-Stevens, a chemist with pesticides company American Cyanamid, appeared as a critic of her work *Silent Spring*. White-Stevens stated, "Miss Carson maintains that the balance of nature is a major force in the survival of man, whereas the modern chemist, the modern biologist and scientist, believes that man is steadily controlling nature."[2]

When *Silent Spring* was published in 1962, very few people were aware of the risks of pesticides. DDT had been widely used during World War II (1939–1945) to combat mosquitoes, lice, and other insects. It was hailed as a miracle pesticide that saved thousands of lives from diseases that are spread by insects, such as malaria and typhus. After the war, the chemical industry, with the support of government agencies, extended the use of DDT to the spraying of crops. They believed DDT would greatly increase crop yields by killing pests. Reports soon appeared, however, that linked the

---

Belief in God and Science

In *Silent Spring*, Carson noted that humans have resisted acknowledging they are a part of the environment. She found that, especially since the splitting of the atom, humans believe that they are the ultimate masters of Earth's secrets and, therefore, cannot fully accept that they are also a part of the natural world. Carson compared this modern attitude to the Victorian reluctance to accept Darwin's theory of evolution. In Darwin's theory, all forms of life are connected. Humans and apes, for example, are from a common ancestor species— a concept many Victorians found difficult to accept. Carson, however, found no conflict between her belief in evolutionary theory and her belief that God was the creator of the universe. She wrote in a letter to James E. Bennet,

Believing as I do in evolution, I merely believe that is the method by which God created, and is still creating, life on earth. And it is a method so marvelously conceived that to study it in detail is to increase . . . one's reverence and awe both for the Creator and the process.[3]

---

crop spraying to the deaths of farm animals, birds, and even people.

By 1958, crop yields were up, but songbirds were dying across the United States. Carson read a letter from a woman that described the sudden deaths of songbirds on her land. DDT had been sprayed on her property, a bird sanctuary, to kill mosquitoes. Earthworms had eaten leaves from the trees that were sprayed. When robins and other species of songbirds ate these earthworms, they were poisoned and died. In addition, the U.S. national bird, the bald eagle, nearly became extinct after many of the birds ate fish contaminated with DDT.

Humans Should Not Control Nature

Carson's response to White-Stevens is well summarized in a paragraph from chapter 17 of *Silent Spring*: "The 'control of nature' is a phrase conceived in arrogance, born of a Neanderthal age of biology and philosophy, when it was supposed that nature exists for the convenience of man. The concepts and practices of applied entomology [insect control] for the most part date from that Stone Age of science. It is our alarming misfortune that so primitive a science has armed itself with the most modern and terrible weapons, and that in turning them against the insects it has also turned them against the earth."[4]

A Difficult Job

Reports of these bird deaths reinforced Carson's longstanding fears about DDT. She decided to bring the threat of pesticides to wider public attention. Carson knew her task would not be easy. The billion-dollar chemical industry would likely attack her if she questioned the usefulness of its products. Because farmers welcomed pesticides as a way to increase the yield of their crops, they might criticize her too. Even some of Carson's readers, including her closest friend, wondered if she should take up a subject that might cause such a stir.

Carson, however, had courage in her convictions. She also knew the power of the printed word. Her book published in 1951, *The Sea Around Us*, had sold hundreds of thousands of copies and was on the best-seller list for 86 weeks. Because of the birds and animals she loved so much, Carson knew that she could not stay silent about the dangers of DDT. Such a silence would violate not only her scientific vow to uncover the truth but also insult her reverence for life.

Preparing the Case

As a scientist, Carson knew that facts must strongly support her case. She included in *Silent Spring* more than 50 pages of references to back up her claims about the effects of DDT and other chemicals. Many of these studies described the effects of pesticides on humans, which included nausea, aching limbs, extreme fatigue, and even cancer.

In 1947, a plane sprayed a California field with DDT to prevent pests from ruining alfalfa crops.

OTHER CHEMICALS

Effects of chemicals in other products further supported Carson's concerns about the use of pesticides. Until 1963, aboveground nuclear bomb tests were common, especially after the first hydrogen bomb explosion in 1952. These tests produced fallout that included the radioactive element strontium-90, which later turned up in pasteurized milk. In the late 1950s and early 1960s, the drug thalidomide, prescribed to thousands of pregnant mothers for morning sickness, was found to cause serious birth defects and was withdrawn from the market. Because of events such as these, people were concerned about the safety of products they used. They began to question the purity of the environment and the effect of toxic chemicals on humans, animals, and plant life.

THE REACTION TO *SILENT SPRING*

With the publication of *Silent Spring*, the chemical industry reacted as Carson and her friends had predicted it would—attacking Carson as a hysterical prophet of gloom and doom. The chemical companies portrayed their products as saviors of humanity from a world of hunger and misery. *Silent Spring* made their products appear to be silent killers. Though Carson was careful not to name specific companies in her book, several threatened to sue her and her publishers.

Others questioned Carson's credentials and motives. Lacking a PhD, she was criticized by some scientists as being unqualified in her field. Linking Carson with political protestors of the period, critics accused her of being a Communist or a peace nut. One government bureaucrat even wondered why Carson was so concerned about genetics since she was unmarried and had no children of her own.

Not all reaction to *Silent Spring* was negative. Carson had supporters in the academic and scientific communities. Her editors stood by her, and fellow naturalists spoke out on her behalf. Brave scientists within the government risked their careers to support her. Members of President John F. Kennedy's administration such as Secretary of the Interior Stewart Udall invited Carson to Washington DC to hear her views. Having read prepublication excerpts in the *New Yorker*, President Kennedy even mentioned Carson's book at a press conference.

In the end, the tide of public opinion swung strongly to her side. In a CBS program on *Silent Spring*

Early Concern

Many believe that Carson decided to write *Silent Spring* after reading a copy of a letter to a newspaper editor given to her by a friend in 1958. The letter described the deaths of songbirds following the spraying of her friend's property with DDT. Carson's biographer, Linda Lear, however, has pointed out that Carson said that her concern about DDT went back as far as 1945, when she first read government reports on its dangers.

in April 1963, viewed by some 10 to 15 million people, Carson's critics came across as one-sided, while Carson appeared reasonable. At one moment Carson contended that "basic scientific truths were being compromised to serve 'the gods of profit and production.'"[5] The propesticide forces had been dealt a blow by one woman determined to awaken the nation to the importance of the environment and the threats against it. ⌐

Rachel Carson appeared on CBS in 1963 to speak about Silent Spring and the negative effect pesticides had on the environment.

*A young Rachel Carson, center, with her brother, Robert Jr.,
and sister, Marian, on the Carson homestead in Pennsylvania*

At the Top of
Her Class

Rachel Carson was born on May 27,
1907, in Springdale, Pennsylvania,
as the youngest of three children. As a young girl,
Rachel loved the world of nature. A shy and serious
child, she felt at home in the woods on her family's

65-acre (26-ha) farm in Springdale. The young girl soon became familiar with the plants and animals around her. Rachel's mother, Maria Carson, was a former teacher and encouraged Rachel's interest in nature. They spent many hours exploring the outdoors together. Her father, at times a clerk, salesman, and power plant worker, struggled to provide for his family. Their home, like many rural houses of the period, had no indoor plumbing and was heated only by fireplaces and a coal stove.

Rachel excelled in school, even though her mother often kept her home because of poor weather or fear of contagious disease. Rachel grew up in an era when diseases such as diphtheria, scarlet fever, and polio were common and often fatal. Her mother was an excellent teacher, however, and Rachel usually received top marks in school despite her absences. Realizing that her daughter had unusual talents, Maria Carson took a somewhat protective attitude toward Rachel. In addition to tutoring her at home, the somewhat stern-faced Mrs. Carson carefully assessed each of Rachel's friends before allowing them to play with her.

A Love of Animals

Throughout her life, Rachel's pets were important to her and frequently mentioned in her letters to friends. In her first book, *Under the Sea-Wind*, Carson gave proper names to some of the sea creatures she was writing about to give them more appeal to the reader.

*From a young age, Rachel loved to read.
She often read aloud to her dog, Candy.*

This attitude would persist in some form throughout Rachel's education.

Rachel loved reading about nature. Beatrix Potter's stories of Peter Rabbit and Kenneth Grahame's *The Wind in the Willows* were among her favorites. As she grew older, she enjoyed books by Herman Melville, Joseph Conrad, and Robert Louis Stevenson. These writers often used the sea as their setting or subject. Rachel developed a strong interest in the ocean, even though she would not experience it directly until she was a graduate student.

Rachel also loved to write. With World War I in progress and her older brother, Robert Jr., in the armed services, Rachel's initial stories focused not on nature but on war. At the age of ten, she sent one of her first stories, "A Battle in the Clouds" to *St. Nicholas* magazine, and it won a silver badge. Greatly excited by the recognition, Rachel submitted other stories to the magazine. Her third story received a gold badge. Rachel's fourth story, "A Famous Sea-Fight," resulted in a $10 prize. Within one year, four of her stories had been published. Rachel was well on her way to becoming a writer. As with almost any writer, not every story she submitted was accepted, but Rachel took rejection in stride.

HIGH SCHOOL YEARS

While Rachel was growing up, her family often struggled to make ends meet. As Rachel Carson's biographer Linda Lear wrote, "The Carsons were more often poor than of modest means."[1] Female teachers

"When I Grow Up . . ."

In a speech to a group of women journalists in 1954, Carson recalled how she came to think of herself as a writer. "I can remember no time, even in earliest child-hood, when I didn't assume I was going to be a writer. . . . I read a great deal almost from infancy, and I suppose I must have realized someone wrote the books, and it would be fun to make up stories too."[2]

such as Maria Carson were not allowed to work after they married. Robert Carson's poorly paid jobs selling insurance and working in the local power plant were the sole source of the family's income. Robert Carson often borrowed money to pay his debts. He made some money by selling off small lots of his land, but his prices became too high to attract buyers. The Carsons kept a cow and had a large garden, both of which helped them manage food costs. Maria Carson taught piano at 50 cents per lesson. Rachel often wore homemade clothes. While she was somewhat embarrassed by this situation at first, "by the time she entered high school," Lear wrote, "Rachel had embraced her mother's view that intellect and self-worth were far more important than material possessions or social recognition."[3]

The Carson family's limited income also affected Rachel's two older siblings. Neither Robert Jr. nor Marian ever went beyond the tenth grade. After his service in World War I, Robert Jr. returned to Springdale and, like his father and older sister, worked for the local power plant. Both Robert Jr. and Marian married, but neither marriage lasted. Her siblings' lack of achievement made Rachel's mother even more determined that Rachel continue her education and eventually go to college.

Rachel's local school only instructed classes through tenth grade. So for high school, most of her classmates chose different schools beginning in ninth grade. To save on transportation costs, however, Rachel's mother had her continue at the local school for the first two years of high school. For the last two years, Rachel transferred to Parnassus High

First Writing Award

When Rachel was 15, *St. Nicholas* magazine published her first piece of nature writing. It described a day she spent in the woods with her dog, Pal, looking for birds' nests.

The call of the trail on that dewy May morning was too strong to withstand. The sun was barely an hour high when Pal and I set off for a day of our favorite sport with a lunch-box, a canteen, a note-book, and a camera. Your experienced woodsman will say that we were going birds'-nesting— in the most approved fashion.

The piece later reveals Rachel's growing powers of observation in her descriptions of various birds' nests. Her love of nature is evident throughout, down to the last lines:

The cool of approaching night settled. The wood-thrushes trilled their golden melody. The setting sun transformed the sky into a sea of blue and gold. A vesper-sparrow sang his evening lullaby. We turned slowly homeward, gloriously tired, gloriously happy![14]

School, a few miles away by streetcar. She graduated first in her class of 44 students in 1925. In addition to pursuing her school subjects, Rachel played basketball and field hockey and cheered at pep rallies.

Throughout high school, Rachel's writing abilities continued to grow. In her senior year she wrote "Intellectual Dissipation," an essay that called on her readers to think for themselves rather than to quote famous writers. Rachel would soon have ample opportunity to practice what she preached. In 1925, she headed off to Pennsylvania College for Women in Pittsburgh, Pennsylvania. Her tuition, room, and board were paid for by a combination of scholarships, funds raised by the president of the college, and additional work taken on by her mother. During her time in college, Rachel would find the path that would lead her to a life of science.

*Rachel published several stories before
she graduated high school in 1925.*

Rachel Carson was devoted to her studies as a student at Pennsylvania College for Women from 1925 to 1929.

COLLEGE AND GRADUATE STUDENT DAYS

When Rachel Carson arrived at Pennsylvania College for Women (now called Chatham University) in 1925, a new and important chapter in her life began. It soon became clear to her classmates that Carson's ambitions in life were larger than most of theirs. Women's colleges were common during this period, but women were still expected to make home and family, rather than a career, their main concerns. Students at women's colleges were taught not only the usual school subjects but also how to dress and behave in social situations. Carson did not concern herself too much with these subjects. She chose to concentrate on her studies and her dream of becoming a writer.

FINDING HER NICHE

While Carson's "inner reserve, confidence, and independence were hard to read" for some of her fellow students, Carson soon found her niche among her peers.[1] She played basketball as a substitute player and was a reliable goalkeeper on the field hockey team. Those who got to know her found that what might seem like aloofness was simply a natural sense of reserve. Carson's focus was on her studies, but she soon made several close friends with whom she shared academic and social interests.

Dreams and Browning

In a paper that Carson wrote as a college freshman, she revealed her professional ambitions while quoting the poetry of Robert Browning: "Sometimes I lose sight of my goal, then again it flashes into view, filling me with a new determination to keep the 'vision splendid' before my eyes. I may never come to a full realization of my dreams, but 'a man's reach must exceed his grasp, or what's a heaven for.'"[2]

College Field Hockey

At Pennsylvania College for Women, Carson started out as a substitute on the field hockey team but ended up as the regular goalkeeper. Her concentration helped Carson's team win the school championship in her junior year. Not surprisingly for those who knew her love for animals and her sense of humor, she also provided her team with a goat for a mascot.

While Carson was in college, her mother continued to play an important role in her life. Living only 16 miles (26 km) away, Maria Carson visited Rachel frequently on campus, arriving Saturday morning and often staying all day. She typed her daughter's papers, took an active interest in her studies, and continued to act as a gatekeeper for her social contacts. On some weekends, Carson would visit her mother at home. Some of her classmates were put off by Carson's mother, but Carson regarded her mother as her best friend.

Carson found support for her academic dreams in two of her professors. In English composition, Grace Croff encouraged her to write for the school literary magazine. Later, her biology professor, Mary Scott Skinker, provided such an inspiring role model that Carson switched her major from English to zoology in her junior year. This was a big change for Carson, who had always thought of herself as a writer. But she did not abandon English when she switched to zoology; she had just found a new subject to write about.

To the Sea at Last

When Carson was a junior, Professor Skinker left the college for Johns Hopkins University to work on her PhD. Carson soon made plans to follow her. In spring 1929, Carson graduated magna cum laude from Pennsylvania College for Women. With the help of Skinker's recommendations, Carson received a full-tuition scholarship of $200 to Johns Hopkins for graduate school. She also eagerly accepted a summer job offer as a beginning investigator working with other students and top scientists at the famous Marine Biological Laboratory on the ocean shore at Woods Hole, Rhode Island.

Carson had never been to the ocean before, but once there she would soon discover the sea was truly her element. Woods Hole could not have been a better place for 22-year-old Carson to be introduced to the wonders of the ocean.

A Crazy Change

Knowing that Carson was a talented writer, her classmate Margaret Wooldridge Fifer advised her against switching majors, saying, "Anyone who can write as well as you can is nuts to switch to biology!"[3]

Carson at Woods Hole in 1929

Carson roomed with her friend, Mary Frye, from Pennsylvania College for Women. She got to know senior scientists in the lab and researched possible subjects for a master's thesis in the library. She absorbed all she could about the ocean, spending hours exploring sea life along the shoreline. According to Linda Lear, "There is no doubt that the genesis of all Carson's sea books, but particularly

The Sea Around Us, belongs to this first summer at Woods Hole."[4]

THE CHALLENGE OF A THESIS

Graduate work at Johns Hopkins was a big change from Pennsylvania College for Women and Woods Hole. The emphasis on research and pursuit of advanced degrees left Carson little time for any social life. Also, the work at Johns Hopkins was more demanding. Her previous classes had stressed general knowledge. Carson's gift had always been to explain clearly and poetically the web of interrelationships between living things and their environment. Now she was expected to specialize.

Carson did very well in her course work. Her master's thesis, however, dealt with a primitive form of the kidney in catfish—hardly a topic to inspire poetic writing. As always, Carson gave it her best effort, but the reactions from her professors were mixed. Carson's adviser praised her review of the articles on catfish and her laboratory findings. Another professor noted that she was a hard worker who knew her biology but implied that she would not make a distinguished research scientist.

RESPONSIBILITY AND WRITING

Carson had always planned to be a teacher rather than a researcher, so these comments may not have upset her too much. What was more upsetting was the job market. The Great Depression had begun in 1929, just as Carson began graduate school. That made finding work more difficult for the other members of the Carson family in Springdale. Carson concluded that the best solution was to move the family to the Baltimore, Maryland, area where she was going to school. Jobs were more plentiful there. They also could save on expenses by living together.

First Comprehensive Look at the Sea World

As a 22-year-old summer student at the Marine Biology Laboratory at Woods Hole, Rhode Island, Carson had a chance to view marine life up close for the first time. Students could go out into Vineyard Sound or Buzzards Bay on a dredging boat. The boat would scoop up marine life from the sea depths and deposit its load of interesting creatures, shells, and seaweed on the boat deck. She later recalled,

Most of these animals I had never seen before; some I had never heard of. But there they were before me. Probably that was when I first began to let my imagination go down under the water and piece together bits of scientific fact until I could see the whole life of those creatures as they lived them in that strange sea world.[5]

Later expeditions would take her below the surface of the water in a diving bell off the coast of Florida and onto a deep-sea dredging vessel much farther off the coast of New England. Yet it was her first dredging trip at Woods Hole that she would remember most fondly.

The new arrangement was initially successful. Maria Carson ran the house. Carson's scholarship and earnings as a summer school lab assistant paid for the family's other expenses. In her second year, however, Carson's earnings did not cover an unexpected tuition increase. She gave up her scholarship and became a part-time student, while working as a part-time lab assistant in the School of Hygiene and Public Health at Johns Hopkins. Carson's household now included her parents, her sister, Marian, who was sometimes too ill with diabetes to work, and Marian's two children. Her brother, Robert Jr., had moved out of the house but was not a dependable source of income for the family.

Shortly after the family moved to Baltimore, Carson's father collapsed and died just outside their home at the age of 71. Maria shipped the body back to her sister-in-law's family in Pennsylvania for burial. There was no money for Maria to travel to her husband's burial service. Carson became even more responsible for the finances of the household.

A Determined Scientist

Carson was always a serious student. Her determination shows in a line from a letter she wrote to her college friend Mary Frye in 1930: "The lab is my world and is going to be my chief existence until I get my degree."[6]

Carson received her master's degree in 1932.
However, financial responsibilities forced her to
drop out of the PhD program in 1934 and seek a
teaching position.

Around this time, she decided to rekindle her
dream to be a writer by sending some of her best
college efforts to magazines. She received nothing
but rejections, yet she was pleased to find that she still
enjoyed writing. Carson began to realize that science
and writing could be joint passions in her life. ―

*Carson's parents visiting her at
Pennsylvania College for Women in 1926*

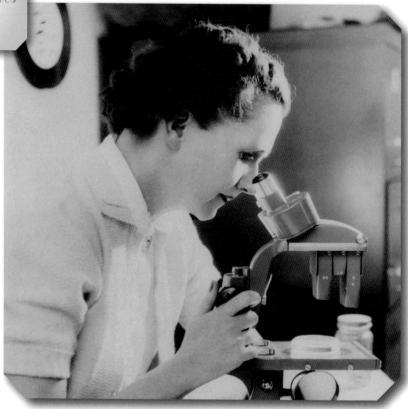

Carson turned her gift for science into a career at the Bureau of Fisheries.

COMBINING SCIENCE
AND WRITING

arson was now the main breadwinner for her family. She needed a regular job, not just part-time teaching and lab assistant assignments. But jobs were hard to come by in 1935 as the Great Depression continued. Her mentor and friend from college, Mary Skinker, advised her to take the federal civil service exams in zoology. Coached by her former professor, Carson took the tests for several positions in biology, including junior wildlife biologist. Her score put her at the top of the list of female applicants. Skinker also advised Carson to contact Elmer Higgins at the Bureau of Fisheries. Carson had previously asked Higgins about possible careers in science for women, but Higgins had not been encouraging. He remarked that science jobs usually went to men. There were no laws against gender discrimination at that time.

Carson took Skinker's advice. This time, Higgins was more open-minded. Perhaps his change of heart was due to an urgent problem. His department was responsible for writing 52 seven-minute scripts for a radio program series about fish behavior. The series was jokingly called "seven-minute fish tales" by the department staff, but none of them could make the topics sound interesting to listeners. Could Carson do any better? She explained that she had begun college as an English major and had published several pieces in the college literary magazine. Higgins decided to give Carson the opportunity. "I've never seen a written word of yours," Carson later remembered Higgins saying, "but I'm going to take a sporting chance."[1]

SEVEN-MINUTE FISH TALES

The part-time assignment was a turning point in Carson's life. Two days a week for eight months, Carson wrote engaging descriptions of sea life, combining what she had learned in her biology and zoology classes with her own personal experiences at Woods Hole. Listeners were intrigued, Elmer Higgins was greatly relieved, and Carson had found her calling. Encouraged by the response to her work, she recycled her research for Higgins into a series of articles on marine life in Chesapeake Bay for the *Baltimore Sun*. Her first article, "It'll Be Shad Time Soon," paid Carson $20 for 12 pages about the decline in local fishing of a saltwater food fish related to the herring. The author's name was "R. L. Carson." In the male-dominated world of science, she and her supervisors agreed that her pieces would be taken more seriously if they appeared to be written by a man.

Writing Not Abandoned

In 1954, Carson described her decision to switch her college major from English to zoology. She noted that "the decision for science was made; the writing courses were abandoned. I had given up writing forever, I thought. It never occurred to me that I was merely getting something to write about."[2]

Higgins's next assignment for Carson was to write an 11-page introduction to a brochure about the sea. Carson gave her essay, "The World of Waters," her best effort, but her boss rejected it, advising her to send it instead to the *Atlantic Monthly*. Higgins's "rejection" was actually a compliment, for the *Atlantic Monthly* was a highly regarded literary magazine. Whether Carson really trusted Higgins's belief in the piece's literary merit is unknown, but she waited more than a year before finally submitting it to the *Atlantic Monthly* editor.

RACHEL CARSON, JUNIOR AQUATIC BIOLOGIST

The Bureau of Fisheries posted a job notice for a junior aquatic biologist. Carson applied and was hired, effective August 17, 1936. She was only one of two professional women in the bureau. It was the beginning of a 15-year career for Carson as a government scientist. She analyzed data, wrote reports, and

Persistence to Publish

Carson was hesitant to submit her work to magazines. Her attempts to interest *Reader's Digest* in a piece on oysters were turned down. The magazine also dismissed a piece about the chimney swift because it already had enough articles on nature at the time. Noting *Reader's Digest* interest in science articles, Carson applied for a staff position but was not hired. Finally, her suggestion that the magazine consider an article on DDT was rejected as too distasteful. She nevertheless persisted and was sometimes rewarded for her efforts.

Carson during her time as an aquatic biologist at the Bureau of Fisheries

produced brochures on fish conservation. She was
promoted within six months and eventually directed
the bureau's publication program. Her work

involved consulting with experts, visiting field sites,
and doing lab work and library research. Carson
enjoyed the challenge of translating the technical
language of scientists into words that the common
reader could understand.

Just when Carson had relieved her immediate
financial problems, tragedy struck. Her sister Marian
came down with pneumonia and died at the age of
40. Carson, not yet 30, and her mother, nearing
70, were left to raise Marian's two children, Virginia
and Marjorie, ages 12 and 11.

Taking charge of the situation, Carson decided
to move the family to a house closer to her office
in Baltimore. Even though the rent was more, the
schools were better, and the move would save on
commuting time. Anticipating more expenses,
Carson also decided at last to send "The World of
Waters" to the *Atlantic Monthly*. A month later, she
received the response of *Atlantic Monthly* editor Edward
Weeks:

> We have everyone of us been impressed by your uncommonly
> eloquent little essay. . . . The findings of science you have
> illuminated in such a way as to fire the imagination of the
> layman.[3]

Expanding "The World of Waters"

Weeks offered Carson $100 for the four-page essay. It appeared in the September 1937 issue.

This was her first piece of nature writing to appear in a well-known national magazine for adults. Carson later said that from these four pages all her later successes followed. Indeed, almost immediately Quincy Howe, the senior editor at Simon & Schuster, a large publishing house in New York City, wrote to Carson. He asked if she had considered expanding her article into a book about the sea.

A Way with Words

In the opening paragraph of "Undersea" (the final published title of "The World of Waters"), Carson not only entices the reader with a question but gives a masterful summary of the entire essay in just a few carefully crafted sentences:

Who has known the ocean? Neither you nor I, with our earth-bound senses, know the foam and surge of the tide that beats over the crab hiding under the seaweed of his tide-pool home; or the lilt of the long, slow swells of mid-ocean, where shoals of wandering fish prey and are preyed upon, and the dolphin breaks the waves to breathe the upper atmosphere. Nor can we know the vicissitudes of life on the ocean floor, where the sunlight, filtering through a hundred feet of water, makes but a fleeting, bluish twilight, in which dwell sponge and mollusk and starfish and coral, where swarms of diminutive fish twinkle through the dust like a silver rain of meteors, and eels lie in wait among the rocks. Even less is it given to man to descend those six incomprehensible miles into the recesses of the abyss, where reign utter silence and unvarying cold and eternal night.[4]

Carson liked the idea. She soon agreed to submit an outline and several chapters.

Combining the research for the book with a vacation, Carson took her mother and two nieces to a beach in North Carolina for ten days. Her excitement at her discoveries was evident to readers when *Under the Sea-Wind* was published three years later.

Carson took the unusual approach of trying to imagine what it felt like to be a seabird, fish, or other ocean creature. The first part of the book traces the amazing life of a shore bird called the sanderling, which may travel some 8,000 miles (13,000 km) each year from the tip of South America to the Arctic Circle. The second part of the book follows a mackerel from its beginnings as an egg floating in the open sea to its catch as an adult fish in a fisherman's net. The last section traces the life of an eel, including its

Literary Science Writing

Many readers compare Rachel Carson's prose to poetry. The rhythmic phrasing of her sentences sometimes suggests the very motion of the sea that she often described in her work. In the introduction to *Under the Sea-Wind*, Carson wrote:

"To stand at the edge of the sea, to sense the ebb and the flow of the tides, to feel the breath of a mist moving over a great salt marsh, to watch the flight of shore birds that have swept up and down the surf lines of the continents for untold thousands of years, to see the running of the old eels and the young shad to the sea, is to have knowledge of things that are as nearly eternal as any earthly life can be."[5]

Carson's Empathy

As a scientist, Carson generally was careful to keep her feelings to herself when writing about nature. She also took pains not to attribute human emotions to animals. That did not mean, however, that Carson lacked such feelings. Throughout her life, she had a strong sense of empathy with all of nature's creatures. For example, Carson described her feelings in a letter to a friend when she saw the hordes of young mullets, a type of fish, swimming against the tidal current to reach the sea: "I stood knee-deep in that racing water and at times could scarcely see those darting silver bits of life for my tears."[6]

birth far below the sea's surface and its 1,000-mile (1,609 km) journey through the Sargasso Sea on the way to the bays and estuaries along the U.S. shores of the Atlantic Ocean.

Despite Carson's best efforts and glowing reviews, sales of *Under the Sea-Wind* were disappointing, perhaps due to current events. One month after the book's November 1941 release, the Japanese attacked Pearl Harbor. The nation turned its full attention to World War II. Carson would wait almost ten years before her name would appear on the best-seller lists.

Carson detailed the habits of several marine creatures, including the migration of sanderlings, in Under the Sea-Wind.

Carson returned to Woods Hole in 1950 for more research and writing.

RISING THROUGH
THE RANKS

During World War II, Carson wanted to contribute to the civilian effort. She trained to be an air raid warden and took a first aid course. But Carson's main contribution to the war effort was to oversee the publication of a series of booklets promoting fish as an alternative to meat in the diet. Meat was being rationed because of the war. This was a topic she could embrace. If there was anything Carson knew how to do, it was to make the remote world of shellfish inviting to the ordinary person. The four booklets, entitled "Food from the Sea," were published between 1943 and 1945.

One of the advantages of her job was having access to the latest research on animals. Carson's research on the ocean for the fish series also yielded articles about the sea that were published in magazines. In 1944, Carson read the research of two Harvard University scientists that compared radar instruments with how bats fly at night. This led to an article originally entitled "He Invented Radar—Sixty Million Years Ago!" Carson noted that bats used a system very similar to radar to fly at night. She sold the article, now retitled "The Bat Knew It First," to *Collier's* and sold reprint rights to *Reader's Digest*. This was the first article

Knowing What We Eat

In her introduction to the "Food from the Sea" pamphlets published in 1943, Carson wrote, "Before we can try new foods, we must know what they are—something of their nutritive value, where they come from, how market supplies vary with the season. Our enjoyment of these foods is heightened if we also know something of the creatures from which they are derived, and where they live, how they are caught, their habits and migrations."[1]

An advocate of conservation, Carson believed wildlife refuges were important in maintaining ecosystems.

she had been able to sell to *Reader's Digest* after several earlier attempts. She also wrote about the wartime use of milkweed floss instead of kapok as filler for life preservers and sleeping bags.

CONSERVATION IN ACTION

After the war, Carson received approval to produce a series of booklets called "Conservation in Action" about the national wildlife refuge system. This is lands set aside by the government to protect wildlife and the places they live. Today, there are more than 500 such refuges visited by tens of millions of people each year. For Carson, the best parts of the project involved visiting the refuge sites and observing the wildlife.

Also important, however, was the opportunity for Carson to promote her philosophy of conservation for the nonscientific reader. She wanted to explain that different forms of life are interdependent. An example of this concept is the food chain. Phytoplankton, or microscopic plants in the water, are eaten by slightly larger creatures called zooplankton. The zooplankton are then eaten by fish, which in turn are eaten by larger fish, which in turn are eaten by humans. Since plants are at the base of the food chain, the variety and quantities of plants available determine the number and kinds of higher forms of life that can thrive.

Back from the Field

Shirley Briggs, a colleague and friend of Carson, described their return from a field trip to Chincoteague National Wildlife Refuge in 1946: "We presented quite a spectacle on our return to the hotel . . . when we came lumbering through, wearing old tennis shoes, usually wet, sloppy and be-smudged pants, various layers of jackets, sou'westers, and toting all manner of cameras. . . ."[2]

The more kinds of plants that are available, the more kinds of animals can survive. Since certain animals depend on certain plants, the removal of any plant could threaten the survival of an animal. Pandas, for example, depend on bamboo to survive. If bamboo forests were eliminated, pandas would likely decrease in number or become extinct.

Carson studied these concepts, which were part of the emerging field of ecology. Today, ecology is understood as the study of the interrelationships among all forms of life and their environments. Many scientists insisted that the ecosystems formed by living things and their environments were only as big as the sum of their parts. Carson believed, however, that ecosystems were actually bigger than the sum of their parts and were constantly changing through interaction with each other.

Not Yet Ecology

The term *ecology* was first coined in 1869, but the concept was not widely used until the 1960s. According to her biographer Linda Lear, Carson did not publicly identify herself as an ecologist until her last major speech at the Kaiser Symposium in 1963. She stated, "It is from the viewpoint of an ecologist that I wish to consider our modern problems of pollution."[3]

DEVELOPING A LIFE-CENTERED PHILOSOPHY

Mark H. Lytle, a Carson biographer, wrote that Carson "wanted to overcome the human-centered view of nature that most Americans held."[4] From her mother, Carson had absorbed a religious point of view that emphasized the wonder and spiritual value of all living things, not just humans. Maria Carson's children studied nature not only firsthand, but also in books written by Anna Botsford Comstock that described a view of nature in which humans were not the only major form of life.

As Carson thought more about what she had seen and read, she began to think about writing a natural history of the seas in which she could expand on the sense of wonder she had first felt at Woods Hole. By September 1948, she was openly discussing the project with colleagues. As usual, however, she faced two major problems: money and time. She had no source for the extra money that would be needed to research such a huge subject. Most of Carson's earnings from her

The Mystery of Nature

The puzzle of nature is a theme to which Carson returns throughout her books and speeches. Near the end of *The Sea Around Us*, she writes, "Even with all our modern instruments for probing and sampling the deep ocean, no one now can say that we shall ever resolve the last, the ultimate mysteries of the sea."[5]

government job went to care for her aging mother, pay the rent on their house, and support her nieces. In addition, her duties at the Bureau of Fisheries left few free hours to work on the book.

Hiring a Literary Agent

A former colleague suggested that Carson hire a literary agent. Literary agents are people who handle the business side of a writer's life. They contact possible publishers, obtain rights and permissions for previously published work, and seek out ways a writer can make money and save time. In Marie Rodell, Carson found someone who excelled at doing all of these things. Rodell quickly eased Carson's financial needs by suggesting Carson apply for a Saxton Fellowship. The money Carson received from the fellowship enabled her to take a four-month leave from her job to focus on research and writing. One trip took her to Florida, where she made her first descent in a diving bell. Poor weather hampered her efforts, but the event still made a lasting impression on Carson. No longer would she have to rely only on her imagination to express how life underwater appears to a fish. Accompanied by Rodell, Carson made a trip on a deep-sea trawler off the coast of New England to take part in a census of sea life.

With Rodell's help, Carson negotiated a contract with Oxford University Press for a book on the natural history of the sea. Carson received a $1,000 advance, with 10 percent deducted for Rodell's fee. The writing schedule was tight, but Carson had always been a disciplined, if slow, writer. When she finally delivered the manuscript of *The Sea Around Us* to Oxford, Carson and Rodell turned their attention to other ways she could make money from her book. When Carson found out she had been selected for a Guggenheim

Finding the Best Title

Finding a title that best fits the subject matter and scope of a book can be a tricky process. Ideally, a book title should accurately suggest the book's content and excite the reader's curiosity. According to Carson's Houghton Mifflin editor, Paul Brooks,

A score of possible titles were considered, debated, discarded: "Return to the Sea," "Mother Sea," "Biography of the Sea," "The Story of the Sea," "Empire of the Sea" and on and on . . .[6]

To relieve the tension at not being able to come up with just the right phrase, Carson's friends and relatives humorously suggested titles such as "Out of My Depth" and "Carson at Sea." Finally, Carson wrote her editor at Oxford University Press: "We have made so many suggestions that I am afraid we have lost track—did we ever mention 'The Sea Around Us'?"[7] Brooks noted, "It had been mentioned once. Now, on second look, it seemed by far the best choice. So at last the matter was settled."[8]

Fellowship, she was thrilled. She was even more amazed when editor William Shawn of the *New Yorker* offered her $7,200 to condense nine of the book's 14 chapters in three prepublication installments. In one sale, she had made more money than her entire annual government salary. Little did she realize that the best news was yet to come. ⌒

Carson's second book, The Sea Around Us, *proved Carson was more than a one-hit wonder in the literary world.*

With the success of The Sea Around Us, *Carson was asked to take on more writing and speaking engagements.*

BEST-SELLING AUTHOR

When *The Sea Around Us* was published on July 1, 1951, Rachel Carson's life changed forever. Enthusiastic reviews appeared in both popular and scientific journals. She was given many honors and awards. The book quickly began to appear on best-seller lists, including in the *New York Times*, where it stayed for 86 weeks—unusual for a book on a scientific subject. Carson was asked to take on projects she once would not have dreamed of. These included writing program notes for a concert of music about the sea and writing the script for a documentary film based on her book. Almost overnight, it seemed, Carson had turned from a government bureaucrat and writer into a well-known personality. Her public appearances were sometimes described in media articles. She was besieged with offers to give speeches. As a naturally shy person, Carson wavered between wanting to spread the word about her book and dreading the idea of speaking in front of groups.

The Shower of Recognition

The reviews must have given her some courage, for they were almost all positive. Carson was pleased about the reviews, for they meant the book would be purchased, making money

A Positive Review

Reviewing *The Sea Around Us* in the *New York Times*, reviewer Jonathan Norton Leonard wrote, "Each of Miss Carson's chapters is worth sampling and savoring, and her book adds up to enjoyment that should not be passed by. Every person who reads it will look on the sea with new pleasure. He will know that it is full of lights and sounds and movements, of sunken lands and mountains, of the debris of meteors, of plains strewn with ancient sharks' teeth and the ear-bones of whales."[1]

*Carson, right, with the poetry and fiction National
Book Award winners in 1952*

that was needed to support her family. She was even
happier to receive the praise of scientists in the field
whom she respected, such as Henry Bigelow, curator
of Harvard's Museum of Comparative Zoology, and
Austin H. Clark, a marine zoologist and curator at
the U.S. National Museum.

Equally exciting were the awards received for *The
Sea Around Us*. Even before the book was published,

Carson's agent had submitted "The Birth of an Island," one chapter from the book, to the American Association for the Advancement of Science for award consideration. In December 1950, Carson was awarded $1,000 by the association for excellence in science writing. The buzz about the upcoming serialization in the *New Yorker* also increased interest in the book. As a result, *The Sea Around Us* was listed as a Book of the Month Club alternate, which guaranteed increased sales after publication. Eventually, the book won the National Book Award for nonfiction. Of all these awards, however, Carson felt the most pride in winning the Burroughs Medal for excellence in nature writing. Her name would now be linked with other great nature writers such as John Burroughs, W. H. Hudson, and Henry David Thoreau.

RACHEL CARSON IN PUBLIC

In the face of this public acclaim, Carson gradually gave up some of her privacy and became more accustomed to signing books in bookstores and making speeches. Nervous at her first major speech, she took the attention

Carson's Findings

Commenting on *The Sea Around Us*, oceanographer and museum director Henry Bigelow noted, "Although I have been concerned with the sea for fifty years, you have found a good many facts I hadn't." [2]

off herself by playing recordings of shrimps, whales, and other fish. She spoke softly but knowledgably. Carson's listeners were impressed with her ability to make events that occurred hundreds of millions of years earlier seem as real as yesterday. Speaking to a group of New York newspaper and book editors and authors, Carson described her experience with the sea snails known as periwinkles. She noted that, like other creatures, these ancient sea creatures were following the pattern of evolution by gradually making a transition from sea life to land life. She went on to describe three types of periwinkles, each at a different stage of transition from land to sea. She concluded her brief science lesson by emphasizing the sea not as a laboratory but as a place of mystery.

The Power of Music

Carson cultivated her "unscientific side" by playing recordings of music for relaxation and for stimulation of new ideas. She had no special training in music, though her mother had taught piano and undoubtedly passed on her interest to her youngest daughter. While listening to Beethoven and Mendelssohn, Carson was inspired to persevere in her efforts to keep the land around her cottage in Maine, a home she later purchased, from being developed.

In 1962, she completed her last book, *Silent Spring*, and received William Shawn's high praise by telephone. For the first time, she realized the book that she had worked so hard on might be a success. That evening she played Beethoven. "And suddenly the tensions of four years were broken," she wrote the next day.[3]

"I doubt that the last, final mysteries of the sea will ever be resolved," she said. "In fact, I cherish a very unscientific hope that they will not be."[4]

FINANCIAL SECURITY

The success of *The Sea Around Us* did not change Carson's basic personality or philosophy. It did, however, relieve the financial pressure she felt as the main provider for her mother and two nieces. Carson was now confident that she could support her family through her books, articles, and other projects. She made plans to quit her government job and become a full-time writer. Already she was planning her next book, which would focus on the kinds of life found by the edge of the sea. The book would enable Carson to do the kind of research she enjoyed most: the inquisitive beachcombing that she had been doing since she initially discovered the wonders of the sea firsthand at Woods Hole.

"People everywhere are desperately eager for whatever will lift them out of themselves and allow them to believe in the future. I am sure that such release from tension can come through the contemplation of the beauties and mysterious rhythms of the natural world."[5]

—*Rachel Carson, 1951*

Dreams and Responsibilities

Even as her fame led her to dream of new
projects, Carson faced another unexpected turn.
Her unmarried niece Marjorie became pregnant. In
1951, the disgrace attached to having a child out of
wedlock could last a lifetime. Carson and her mother
were able to keep the situation from becoming widely
known. Born in 1952, Roger would be the source
of much joy (and some pain) to both Marjorie and
Carson.

The problems caused by Marjorie's situation
may have spoiled much of the joy that Carson
would have experienced in her newfound literary
success. However, the woman who had already
spent a large part of her life caring for her parents,
siblings, and nieces now took on, without hesitation,
the additional financial responsibility for her
grandnephew. One could only wonder whether
there were limits to Carson's ability to shoulder the
burdens of others while maintaining the increasing
responsibilities of her own life. ⌐

One of Carson's favorite activities was exploring
seashores for interesting creatures.

Carson and a coworker searched for sea creatures along the shore of the Florida Keys in 1952.

BY THE EDGE OF THE SEA

s *The Sea Around Us* made its way up the best-seller lists, Carson was already working on her next book, *The Edge of the Sea*.

The idea for the book had come about when a Houghton Mifflin editor was walking along a beach with a group of friends. They came across a number of horseshoe crabs that seemed to be stranded after a storm. The visitors thought to do the crabs a favor by returning them to the sea. They later learned the crabs were purposely on shore for mating purposes. After returning to her office, the editor proposed that Carson write a book that would correct the general reader's ignorance of basic seashore life.

A Guide to Discovery

The project started out as a small handbook that would give the reader information to understand life on the edge of the sea, but it soon evolved into something more. Carson came to the conclusion that the seashore, like the sea, is best described as a total environment with various strands of interrelated life. With this new concept, she reorganized *The Edge of the Sea* around three distinct kinds of seashores.

In planning her research in Maine, Carson hoped to use some of her earnings from *The Sea Around Us* to buy a house so she could be near the sea during the summer months. In 1953, she found an area overlooking an estuary of the Sheepscot River on Southport Island near Boothbay Harbor. The river was so deep and rich with life that whales, seals, and a variety of tidal pool life were all on view. It was a perfect setting for Carson's favorite activity: hunting for sea creatures. Since there was no appropriate house in the vicinity, she decided to build her own. The house would have a sun deck, screened porch, room for her mother, and a study space for her books, microscope, and other materials. It would be her summer home for the rest of her life.

The Beginnings of a Lifelong Friendship

Perhaps the best result of Carson's choice for her summer home was her new next-door neighbors, Dorothy and Stanley Freeman. Carson and Dorothy Freeman had much in common. Although Freeman was not a professional naturalist, she took a keen interest in the natural world. Freeman had read *The Sea Around Us* when it first came out and was quite excited that its author was now living next door. Carson found special pleasure in showing Freeman the

Three Kinds of Seashores

Three national parks provide examples of the kinds of seashores in *The Edge of the Sea*:
• Acadia National Park, Bar Harbor, Maine, has 45,000 acres (18,000 ha) of rocky coasts, ocean, islands, and forest in ecosystems ranging from intertidal to subalpine.
• Cape Hatteras National Seashore, Manteo, North Carolina, has more than 30,000 acres (12,000 ha) of seashore in an area rich with both human and natural history.
• Biscayne National Park, Homestead, Florida, has 175,000 acres (71,000 ha) of living coral reefs, snorkeling, and scuba diving—all within sight of nearby Miami.

wonders of the tide pools near their homes. After they returned to their respective winter homes at the end of the summer, they continued their friendship by mail. During the next 12 years, Carson and Freeman exchanged more than 750 letters. These letters fill more than 500 pages of *Always, Rachel,* a volume later edited by Freeman's granddaughter. In her older neighbor, Carson found a friend with whom she could share her deepest feelings.

ANOTHER BEST SELLER

Although not as spectacularly successful as *The Sea Around Us, The Edge of the Sea* was a best seller for almost five months and won several awards.

Bringing the Shore to Life

In the beginning paragraph of *The Edge of the Sea,* Carson provides a general picture of her subject, but also gives specific details that sharpen the reader's interest in finding out more about the seashore's changing character:

The edge of the sea is a strange and beautiful place. All through the long history of Earth it has been an area of unrest where waves have broken heavily upon the land, where the tides have pressed forward over the continents, receded, and then returned. For no two successive days is the shore line precisely the same. Not only do the tides advance and retreat in their eternal rhythms, but the level of the sea itself is never at rest. It rises or falls as the glaciers melt or grow, as the floor of the deep ocean basins shifts . . . or as the earth's crust along the continental margins warps up and down. . . . Today a little more land may belong to the sea, tomorrow a little less. Always the edge of the sea remains an elusive and indefinable boundary.[2]

Its success was due largely to Carson's personal approach to her subject.

At age 48, with two best sellers to her credit and the promise of more projects to come, Carson's life seemed to be a source of envy. Yet even supportive friends and stimulating work could not prevent events beyond her control from intruding on her happiness. In just a few short years, the frailty of her aging mother and the health problems of her niece Marjorie would present Carson with the greatest challenges she had yet faced.

Guiding the Reader

Reviewing *The Edge of the Sea* in 1955 for the *Saturday Review,* one critic noted, "Though Rachel Carson does not literally take the reader by the hand, she is always close by, looking into tide pools, walking along sandy beaches, or clambering over slippery weed-covered rocks."[3]

Carson reading and writing in the woods near her home in 1962

Carson enjoyed teaching children about the wonders of nature.

DREAMS AND REALITIES

The time around the publication of *The Edge of the Sea* was one of the happiest periods in Carson's life. Its success helped her to look optimistically to the future, at least for a while. Chatham College, her recently renamed alma mater,

presented her with a Distinguished Alumnae Service
Award. The American Association of University
Women gave her a $2,500 Achievement Award.
She happily plunged into research for a short book
on evolution and approved the concept of a junior
edition of *The Sea Around Us* for children. Carson
also agreed to write a magazine article on how to
introduce children to the natural world. "Help Your
Child to Wonder" was based on her adventures in
Maine with her grandnephew, Roger.

She also produced a script for a television show
about clouds called "Something About the Sky."
An eight-year-old viewer who had written CBS
about her curiosity of the sky had suggested the
subject. Carson did not own a television when she
wrote the script. She watched the final production
at her brother's house and was so pleased with the
results that she soon bought her own television.
The purchase made both Carson's mother and
grandnephew happy.

New writing projects and awards, however,
could not help Carson forget the worsening health
problems of her mother and her niece Marjorie.
Maria Carson's crippling arthritis grew worse and
made Carson's care more necessary. Marjorie's

diabetes meant that her son, Roger, also became more of Carson's responsibility.

The Vision of the Lost Woods

Still, Carson found the energy to pursue another dream: to purchase a piece of land called the Lost Woods near her house in Maine. Carson wanted to turn the land into a nature preserve. She hoped to raise enough funds through her writing and others' contributions to convince the owner to sell the land so that it could be left undeveloped. To help finance the project, Carson planned an anthology of articles about the relationship humans have with their environment. She had to abandon that project and the dream of her Lost Woods, however, when Marjorie died suddenly of pneumonia at the age of 31 in 1957. Carson now became the primary caregiver for Roger, who was five years old.

The Lost Woods

In a 1956 letter to a friend, Carson described her fascination with the large tract of land near her summer home that she was determined to preserve. "[The Lost Woods'] charm for me lies in its combination of rugged shore rising in rather steep cliffs for the most part, and cut in several places by deep chasms where the storm surf must create a magnificent scene. . . . Behind this is the wonderful, deep, dark woodland—a cathedral of stillness and peace. . . . It is a treasure of a place to which I have lost my heart, completely."[1]

Despite being almost 50 years old, Carson realized that she was now the person to whom Roger felt closest. She decided the best choice was to adopt him, which she did in 1957. While she accepted her new role, Carson knew her decision would make great demands on her time and energies. She hired a housekeeper to help her run the house in Maryland but could find no one to help with childcare while she was in Maine. Stanley and Dorothy Freeman did what they could, but Carson still cared for Roger a great deal of the time. This left little time for her own work on the junior edition of *The Sea Around Us*.

Roger Christie

Carson's grandnephew, Roger Christie, was born in February 1952 as the only child of Carson's niece Marjorie. After Marjorie's death, Carson did not hesitate to adopt Roger. Yet she knew the job of raising him would not be easy. Carson was financially secure due to the success of *The Sea Around Us*, but she was short on the time and energy needed to raise a child. Roger's sadness at the loss of his mother was expressed in the form of demands for extra attention.

In Roger, however, Carson found an interested companion for her nature walks. "I have been amazed at the way names stick in his mind," Carson wrote in "Help Your Child to Wonder," later published in book form as *The Sense of Wonder*.

For when I show color slides of my woods plants, it is Roger who can identify them. . . . I am sure no amount of drill would have implanted the names so firmly as just going through the woods in the spirit of two friends on an exciting discovery.[2]

*In 1957, Carson adopted her grandnephew, Roger, who also liked
exploring the outdoors.*

TECHNOLOGY VERSUS THE NATURAL WORLD

Without a big writing project in progress when
she and her family returned to Maryland that
fall in 1954, Carson had more time to read the
newspaper and think about current events. Since
1952, widespread nuclear testing had been a concern
for Carson. Now she read about the Soviet Union's

launch of the first intercontinental missile and the successful launch of *Sputnik I* and *II*, the first satellites to orbit Earth. Carson also learned that the U.S. Department of Agriculture was planning a massive new program to try to eliminate the fire ant from the South and Southwest.

For some scientists, these developments represented triumphs of technology. For Carson, however, alarm bells signaled deep concerns about the future of the natural world. What if satellites were used as vehicles of war? What effect would the elimination of the fire ant have on the food chain?

Carson was able to express some of her concerns about the threats to the natural world in an article titled "Our Ever-Changing Shore" that she wrote for *Holiday* magazine. The article combined colorful descriptions of seashores with a plea to preserve these areas against the threat of human overdevelopment.

Society's Destruction

Carson's hero was Albert Schweitzer. The following quotation of his appeared in a 1956 bulletin of the International Union for the Conservation of Nature and Natural Resources: "Modern man no longer knows how to foresee or to forestall. He will end by destroying the earth from which he and other living creatures draw their food."[3]

The words struck Carson with such force that she used the quotation in a proposal to the editor of the *New Yorker* for an article about pesticides.

An Emerging Point of View

Perhaps without consciously
realizing it, Carson's reading and
writing about environmental threats
helped shape her point of view for
her next book, *Silent Spring*. Carson
wanted to believe that the physical
world was ultimately indestructible,
but could not. She wrote to Freeman
that with the beginning development
of atomic weapons,

> *I have now opened my eyes and my
> mind. I may not like what I see, but it
> does no good to ignore it. . . . Man seems
> actually likely to take into his hands—ill-
> prepared as he is psychologically—many
> of the functions of God.*[4]

In spite of many difficulties, these
dramatic developments in Carson's
thinking would drive her to produce
her greatest masterpiece.

Carson exploring the woods behind her home in Maine in 1961

Plant and animal life suffered from direct and indirect spraying of DDT until it was banned in the United States in 1972.

FIGHTING THE BATTLE

In planning and writing *Silent Spring*, Carson called upon all her talents as a literary artist, scientist, and advocate for the public good. Once Carson had drawn in the reader with her dramatic first chapter, "Fable for Tomorrow," she sketched the history and a scientific description of the pesticide DDT.

Many regarded this chemical as a miracle pesticide, but Carson compared it to the harmful radioactive element strontium-90 released by atomic explosions. Both DDT and strontium-90 accumulate in living tissue. In the case of DDT, she noted, insects targeted by the chemical can build up resistance to its effects. New insecticides are then necessary to be effective, but insects soon become immune to these new chemicals as well. The cycle continues, increasing the types and amounts of chemicals collecting on soil and vegetation.

At the time she was writing, Carson noted, almost 500 new chemicals were being introduced in the United States each year, with unknown consequences for the environment. She was careful not to condemn the use of all chemicals and pesticides. Instead, she urged only that they be used selectively and sparingly in order to maintain the

Not Quite Fatal

As an advocate for the public good, Carson warned her readers of the forces that she felt were creating an unhealthy environment. In *Silent Spring*, she quoted the words of ecologist Paul Shepard: "Why should we tolerate a diet of weak poisons, a home in insipid surroundings, a circle of acquaintances who are not quite our enemies, the noise of motors with just enough relief to prevent insanity? Who would want to live in a world which is just not quite fatal?"[1]

balance that had been achieved among the various forms of life on Earth over millions of years.

The Scope of Silent Spring

After describing DDT and related chemicals, *Silent Spring* examined how chemicals affect several major elements of life on Earth—water, soil, plant life, wildlife, birds, and fish. The rest of the book focused on different aspects of the subject of pesticides (or biocides, as Carson preferred to call them, since they do not always discriminate among different forms of life). These suspects included aerial spraying of pesticides, common household and garden chemicals, chemically caused diseases, the effect of chemicals on human cell structure, cancer, natural resistance to chemicals, and alternatives to chemical pesticides.

Water Contamination

Anyone who has ever watered a potted plant and watched how quickly the water can seep through

A Reviewer's Criticism

Most critics gave *Silent Spring* good reviews, but a few, such as *Time* magazine, criticized what they saw as Carson's pro-nature bias: "Many scientists sympathize with Miss Carson's love of wildlife, and even with her mystical attachment to the balance of nature. But they fear that her emotional and inaccurate outburst in *Silent Spring* may do harm by alarming the nontechnical public, while doing no good for the things that she loves."[2]

Carson, far left, *met with the president's Science Advisory Committee in 1963 to discuss threats to the environment.*

the hole in the bottom of the pot can realize how fast insecticides can travel through soil after being sprayed on plants. Once in the soil, insecticides can seep into groundwater that eventually flows into lakes, rivers, and creeks. These deadly chemicals then lodge in the fish that swim in these bodies of water.

Carson cited studies of fish by the U.S. Fish and Wildlife Service that showed two facts. First, fish absorb and retain DDT from the water in their fatty tissue. Second, fish swimming as far as 30 miles (48 km) downstream from the nearest spraying still contained DDT in their tissues. Groundwater was the most likely means of contamination. After examining similar studies, Carson concluded, "It is not possible to add pesticides to water anywhere without threatening the purity of water everywhere."[3]

Emotional but Factual

Carson was accused of being too emotional about wildlife, but there was no denying the facts in the scientific reports she quoted in *Silent Spring*. An example is a report on the effects of insect spraying in 1958 in a trout stream in Maine: "These fish exhibited the typical symptoms of DDT poisoning; they swam erratically, gasped at the surface, and exhibited tremors and spasms. In the first five days after spraying, 668 dead suckers were collected from two blocking nets."[4]

THE SOIL BENEATH US

Humans may take the soil underfoot for granted, but it plays an important role in supporting thousands of forms of life—not just the ones that are visible above the surface. For example, Darwin showed that earthworms help enrich the soil and are crucial in transporting soil from far below the surface to where it is needed by plants. Earthworms that ate leaves sprayed by DDT absorbed the poison. Some died, leaving fewer earthworms to maintain the soil.

Others were eaten by birds. Studies showed a robin could die after eating as few as 11 earthworms that had ingested DDT.

Earthworms contribute to healthy soil, which is necessary to make nitrogen for plants so they can grow properly. Carson cited experiments showing that after only two weeks in the soil, the pesticides lindane and heptachlor reduced the nitrogen available to plants. When sprayed on orchards four times over a single season, up to 113 pounds (51 kg) of DDT residue per acre (.4 ha) can accumulate in the soil under the trees. Carson summarized the dangers by quoting the summary of a conference of soil specialists at Syracuse University:

A Judge's Esteem

Supreme Court Justice William O. Douglas was not only a famous judge and lover of the outdoors, but also a friend of Carson's and a supporter of her work. In his book on the Pacific West, Douglas wrote these words that Carson quoted in *Silent Spring*: "The aesthetic values of the wilderness are as much our inheritance as the veins of copper and gold in our hills and the forests in our mountains."[6]

> *A few false moves on the part of man may result in destruction of soil productivity and the arthropods [a branch of living things without backbones that includes insects, spiders, and crabs] may well take over.*[5]

Tampering with Earth's Green Mantle

Today, most humans are far enough removed
from plant life that they may forget how much
they need plants to survive. Humans, said Carson,
often ignore a crucial fact: one person's weed is
another animal's essential ingredient in the chain
of living things on which humans depend. In the
chapter titled "Earth's Green Mantle," Carson cited
cattlemen on the western plains as an example. For
them, sagebrush was a useless plant that got in the
way of planting the grass needed to feed their cows.
Cattle owners promoted grass and sprayed sagebrush.
They may not have realized that sagebrush also
provided food for deer and antelope and shelter for
game birds such as grouse. The cattlemen also failed
to note that grass requires moisture—something
dispensed more reliably from moisture-holding
sagebrush than from the less reliable rainfall in
the plains states. Because of these characteristics of
sagebrush, eliminating the plant had negative effects
on the cattle herds.

When herbicides are applied to roadsides as
well as fields, the variety of vegetation can decrease.
Carson bemoaned the loss:

[The] disfigurement of once beautiful roadsides by chemical sprays, which substitute a [dry] expanse of brown withered vegetation for the beauty of fern and wildflower, of native shrubs adorned with blossom or berry. [7]

Instead, Carson proposed selective spraying to promote shrubs and other low-lying plants. Small plants would discourage growth of unwanted trees that obscure the driver's vision and interfere with overhead wires. Studies showed that areas so treated required no further spraying for at least 20 years. Carson summarized other alternative solutions in the last chapter of *Silent Spring*.

On Completing *Silent Spring*

Only a few days after she submitted the final manuscript of *Silent Spring* to William Shawn of the *New Yorker*, Carson received a phone call from the legendary editor. Shawn called the work a "brilliant achievement" and described it as "full of beauty and loveliness and depth of feeling."[8] After so many months of hard work, illness, and fear that she would never be able to complete the book, Shawn's words created a "happy turbulence" in Carson. "Suddenly I knew from his reaction that my message would get across," Carson recalled.[9]

After the phone call with Shawn, Carson wrote her friend Dorothy Freeman to share the good news about *Silent Spring*. Carson once told Freeman that she "could never again listen happily to a thrush song" if she had not done all she could to save the natural world from the threat of pesticides. Carson now wrote, "And last night the thoughts of all the birds and other creatures and all the loveliness that is in nature came to me with such a surge of deep happiness, that now I *had* done what I could— I had been able to complete it—now it had its own life!"[10]

The Final Season

Knowing that groups she was criticizing would attack her, Carson carefully researched and documented all her facts in *Silent Spring*. Despite the book's scholarly trappings and its potentially grim message, *Silent Spring* soon appeared on the best-seller lists, where it remained number one for most of the fall of 1962. It ultimately sold more than 500,000 copies and continues to sell well today.

While writing the book, Carson's health declined. She handled smaller illnesses such as sinusitis, flu, and an ulcer with few complaints during this period. But she was also battling cancer. Rachel Carson died on April 14, 1964, at age 56. Her vision and message about the importance of the natural world, however, would continue to inspire others in the coming years. ⌒

In June 1963, Carson testified before the Senate Government Operations Subcommittee about the need to end aerial spraying.

In 1966, the Rachel Carson National Wildlife Refuge was established in Maine to protect land for migrating birds.

THE LEGACY OF RACHEL CARSON

A consumer reaching for a box of organic cereal today may not know who Rachel Carson was. Likewise, TV news viewers watching the latest reports on endangered species or pesticides may have no idea that Carson was among the first

to report on such topics more than
50 years ago. Whether the subject
is pesticides in the soil or pollution
in the air and water, wilderness
preservation or the dangers of
cancer-causing substances in the food
chain, Carson brought these topics
to public attention and became a
pioneer of environmentalism.

FRUITS OF CARSON'S CRUSADE

Within five months of Carson's
death, President Lyndon B. Johnson
signed the Wilderness Act, which
originally protected 9.1 million
acres (3.7 million ha) of federal land
from further development and now
protects more than 106 million acres
(42 million ha). The act defines
wilderness as an area "where the
earth and its continuity of life are
untrammeled by man, where man
himself is a visitor who does not
remain."[1] While Carson had no direct
influence on the Wilderness Act,

Still Harming the Environment

Edward O. Wilson has been a Harvard professor and entomologist for almost 50 years and has written more than 20 books. After considering the state of Earth's environment in his 2007 essay, "On *Silent Spring*," Wilson concluded, "We are still poisoning the air and water and eroding the biosphere, albeit less so than if Rachel Carson had not written."[2]

her writings brought environmental concerns into the public's discussion.

Carson helped inspire governments and individuals to treat the environment with more attention and respect. Outraged by a 1969 oil spill off Santa Barbara, California, Senator Gaylord Nelson of Wisconsin persuaded Congress to designate April 22 as Earth Day. Each year on that date, participants would gather to educate themselves and others about the threats to the environment. The first Earth Day, April 22, 1970, drew 22 million people to various events around the world. That same year, the Environmental Protection Agency (EPA) was established to protect human health and the environment through research, monitoring, standards, and law enforcement. As the national consciousness was raised, Congress passed more laws, including the Clean Water Act of 1972. It was one

International Sales

As of 2007, *Silent Spring* had been published in 23 different editions in the following 17 countries: Brazil, Denmark, Finland, France, Germany, Great Britain, Iceland, Israel, Italy, Japan, the Netherlands, Norway, Portugal, Spain, Sweden, the United States, and the former Yugoslavia.

Populations of some bird species, such as the bald eagle, increased after DDT was banned in 1972.

part of a new type of legislation that allowed citizens to bring lawsuits against polluters. In 2007, the EPA spent approximately $8.7 billion, of which almost half was to ensure clean and safe water.

Within a few years after Carson's death, the newly founded Environmental Defense Fund mounted a series of lawsuits that resulted in the banning of DDT in the United States in 1972. Other insecticides have since replaced DDT, however, and the United States now consumes 50 percent more pesticides than it did in 1964. Nevertheless, the ban on DDT was responsible for the revival of many bird species, including the bald eagle.

Examples of Citizen Involvement

Chemical companies produced not only pesticides but other substances hazardous to humans. Beginning in the 1940s, Hooker Chemical (now part of Occidental Petroleum) began to bury toxic waste in a site on Love Canal, a neighborhood in Niagara Falls, New York. By 1978, suspicious illnesses among children living on Love Canal prompted Lois Gibbs, a local mother, to investigate. That same year, President Jimmy Carter declared a federal emergency at Love Canal. Those living on the site were relocated. But Gibbs led the fight to hold accountable the company that had buried the waste and harmed the community. Her organization, the Love Canal Homeowners Association, found that more than half the children in the area who were born from 1974 to 1978 had birth defects ranging from cleft palates to extra teeth. In 1980, Congress passed the Superfund Act to aid persons and communities harmed by chemical waste. It was not until 1995, however, that the company responsible for poisoning Love Canal agreed to pay $129 million in restitution.

Beginning in 1991, Erin Brockovich fought to expose a California public utility, Pacific Gas and Electric, as the party responsible for covering up the industrial poisoning of a town's water supply. In 2000, the movie based on her story, *Erin Brockovich*, opened in theaters to wide acclaim.

There are more potential threats to the environment today than in Carson's era. These threats include the causes of climate change, increasing world population, the destruction of tropical rain forests, and the growing world demand for more energy. Yet governments around the world, as well as individual citizens, are now more involved in confronting these problems. Just one organization, the

The Power of One

Writing in 1970, at the beginning of the modern environmental movement, anthropologist Margaret Mead emphasized the importance of individual commitment in transforming society: "Never doubt that a small group of thoughtful, committed citizens can change the world; indeed, it is the only thing that ever has."[3]

National Resources Defense Council, founded in 1970 by a small group of law students and attorneys, has 1.2 million members and online activists today. There are many similar organizations in the United States and abroad.

THE CONTINUING ENVIRONMENTAL CHALLENGE

While there is disagreement on how to solve environmental problems, few doubt that such problems exist. For example, there is debate about the seriousness of the climate change

---

DDT and Malaria

Each year, more than 300 million people, mostly in Africa, develop malaria from mosquito bites. More than 1 million people die of the disease. Today, malaria is far worse than it was in Carson's day. Some people suggest this is because DDT use has declined. DDT kills a wide swath of living things, including mosquitoes, which carry malaria. However, use of DDT to decrease malaria is debated, as some mosquitoes have developed a resistance both to DDT and to drugs that were once effective in treating malaria.

It is important to emphasize that, as Linda Lear has noted,

Rachel Carson never called for the banning of DDT and never suggested in Silent Spring that pesticides not be used. Her research suggested that chemical pesticides were being used inefficiently, ineffectively, and indiscriminately.[4]

In Carson's spirit, the current solution favors careful use of DDT only in countries where other solutions are not yet available. These other solutions include indoor residual spraying that targets the walls of homes where mosquitoes rest and insecticide-treated bed nets that protect people who sleep under them.

threat. Some argue that the current warming trend is part of a normal cycle of warming and cooling that Earth has undergone over thousands of years. Lacking the knowledge that scientists now possess from recent studies, Carson put forward that argument in an article she wrote for *Popular Science* in 1951 that was drawn from her best seller, *The Sea Around Us*. Today, however, armed with additional scientific data, many scientists warn that unless atmospheric carbon is reduced, the Arctic icecap could completely melt. The effects could include the loss of untold thousands of species of plants and animals. It could also increase the ocean level and would endanger many shoreline habitats, including many cities.

When Senator Abraham Ribicoff introduced Carson to his subcommittee on environmental hazards in 1963 as "the lady who started all this," he likely did not realize how relevant Carson's warnings would continue to be today.[5] Al Gore's book *Earth in the Balance* (2000) and his Oscar-winning film, *An Inconvenient Truth* (2006), once again have brought climate change to the forefront of public consciousness. Carson had a direct impact on Gore. "*Silent Spring* was one of the books we read at home at my mother's insistence and then discussed around the dinner table," Gore has written. "Indeed, Rachel Carson was one of the reasons why I became so conscious of the environment and so involved with environmental issues."[6]

When Rachel Carson sounded the alarm about the dangers of pesticides, she proved that one person truly can have a significant impact on the world. Today, more Rachel Carsons are stepping forward, as well as volunteers who will support them, as the world faces the continuing environmental challenges of the twenty-first century. ⌐

Through lifelong curiosity, research, and writing, Rachel Carson brought environmental awareness to the public.

TIMELINE

1907	1918	1925
Rachel Carson is born on May 27 in Springdale, Pennsylvania.	Carson's first published story, "A Battle in the Clouds," appears in *St. Nicholas* magazine.	Carson graduates from Parnassus High School.

1937	1941	1949
The *Atlantic Monthly* accepts Carson's story, "The World of Waters."	Simon & Schuster publishes *Under the Sea-Wind*.	Carson becomes chief editor of publications for the U.S. Fish and Wildlife Service.

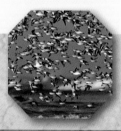

1929	1932	1936
Carson graduates from Pennsylvania College for Women.	Carson receives a master's degree in zoology at Johns Hopkins University.	The Bureau of Fisheries hires Carson as a junior aquatic biologist.

1951	1951	1952
The *New Yorker* publishes the first of a three-part series from *The Sea Around Us*.	Oxford University Press publishes *The Sea Around Us*.	Carson is awarded the Burroughs Medal.

TIMELINE

1955	1956	1962
Houghton Mifflin publishes *The Edge of the Sea*.	CBS airs Carson's episode on clouds.	The first of three installments of *Silent Spring* appears in the *New Yorker* in June.

1964	1970	1970
President Lyndon Johnson signs the Wilderness Act into law.	The first Earth Day is celebrated on April 22 by 22 million participants around the world.	The Environmental Protection Agency is established.

1962	1963	1964
Houghton Mifflin publishes *Silent Spring* in September.	CBS airs "The Silent Spring of Rachel Carson."	Carson dies on April 14 at age 56.

1972	1972	1980
Congress passes the Clean Water Act.	DDT is banned in the United States.	Congress passes the Superfund Act to aid those harmed by chemical waste.

Essential Facts

Date of Birth

May 27, 1907

Place of Birth

Springdale, Pennsylvania

Date of Death

April 14, 1964

Parents

Robert and Maria Carson

Education

Parnassus High School; Pennsylvania College for Women; Johns Hopkins University

Marriage

None

Children

Adopted grandnephew, Roger

Career Highlights

Rachel Carson worked in the Bureau of Fisheries for 15 years. Throughout her life, she wrote several essays and books that brought wider attention to nature and the sea. Her most influential work, *Silent Spring*, raised public awareness of environmental harms.

Societal Contribution

Rachel Carson's most influential book, *Silent Spring*, was instrumental in launching environmentalism. This book demonstrated to the world how harmful DDT and other pesticides can be when they are used incorrectly. This launched legislative action that hindered harmful chemicals and preserved wildlife reserves. In many ways, Carson was a pioneer for today's environmental movement.

Conflicts

Many of Carson's theories about negative effects of chemicals and pesticides on the environment were disputed in her time. After *Silent Spring* was published, chemical companies and others with a vested interest in her work contested the accuracy of her claims in the book and even questioned her capabilities as a scientist.

Quote

"It is our alarming misfortune that so primitive a science has armed itself with the most modern and terrible weapons, and that in turning them against the insects it has also turned them against the earth."—*Rachel Carson, 1962*, Silent Spring

Additional Resources

Select Bibliography

Brooks, Paul. *The House of Life: Rachel Carson at Work*. 1972. Boston, MA: Houghton Mifflin, 1989.

Carson, Rachel. *Silent Spring*. 40th anniversary ed. Boston, MA: Houghton Mifflin, 2002.

Lear, Linda. *Rachel Carson: Witness for Nature*. New York, NY: Henry Holt, 1997.

Lytle, Mark H. *The Gentle Subversive: Rachel Carson, Silent Spring, and the Rise of the Environmental Movement*. New York, NY: Oxford University Press, 2007.

Further Reading

Carson, Rachel. *The Sense of Wonder*. New York, NY: HarperCollins, 1998.

Lear, Linda, ed. *Lost Woods: The Discovered Writing of Rachel Carson*. Boston, MA: Beacon, 1998.

Levine, Ellen. *Up Close: Rachel Carson*. New York, NY: Penguin, 2007.

MacGillivray, Alex. *Rachel Carson's Silent Spring*. Hauppage, NY: Barron's, 2004.

WEB LINKS

To learn more about Rachel Carson, visit ABDO Publishing Company online at **www.abdopublishing.com**. Web sites about Rachel Carson are featured on our Book Links page. These links are routinely monitored and updated to provide the most current information available.

PLACES TO VISIT

Chincoteague National Wildlife Refuge
Chincoteague, VA 23336
757-336-6122
www.fws.gov/northeast/chinco
View some of the 14,000 acres (5,700 ha) of beaches, dunes, marshes, and maritime forests, plus a herd of wild horses.

Rachel Carson Homestead: National Historic Site
613 Marion Avenue, Springdale, PA 15144
724-274-5459
www.rachelcarsonhomestead.org
Tour Rachel Carson's childhood home where she first came to love nature. A gift shop includes her famous books.

Rachel Carson National Wildlife Refuge
321 Port Road, Wells, ME 04090
207-646-9226
www.fws.gov/northeast/rachelcarson
Explore 50 miles (80.5 km) of coastline in Maine's York and Cumberland counties. The Web site includes descriptions of activities in the refuge and excerpts from Carson's writings.

GLOSSARY

algae
Water plants that can make their own food.

bureaucrat
A government official.

DDT
Dichlorodiphenyltrichloroethane; a colorless, odorless insecticide now banned in the United States.

diminutive
Small.

dissipation
Wasting by misusing.

ecology
The study of the interrelationships among all forms of life and their environments.

ecosystem
The relationships among a community of organisms and their environment.

entomology
The study of insects.

estuary
The mouth of a river into which the tide flows.

exultation
Great rejoicing.

heptachlor
A pesticide that causes liver disease in animals and may cause cancer in humans.

horseshoe crab
> A sea animal shaped like a horseshoe with a long, spiny tail.

kapok
> Silky fibers from the seed of the ceiba tree.

lindane
> An insecticide.

mollusk
> Any of a large group of animals, such as snails, with large, unsegmented bodies usually covered with shells.

mullet
> A type of fish that lives in warm waters close to shore.

pesticide
> Something used to kill pests.

restitution
> A legal act meant to restore something to its previous state.

sonar
> A device that emits sound waves underwater to detect objects.

thesis
> A paper written by a person working toward an academic degree.

vicissitude
> A change in fortune or circumstances.

zoology
> The study of animals and animal life.

Source Notes

Chapter 1. Sounding the Alarm

1. Rachel Carson. *Silent Spring*. 40th anniversary ed. Boston, MA: Houghton Mifflin, 2002. 1.
2. *Rachel Carson's Silent Spring*. The American Experience. Writ. and prod. Neil Goodwin. PBS. 1993.
3. Linda Lear. *Rachel Carson: Witness for Nature*. New York, NY: Henry Holt, 1997. 227.
4. Rachel Carson. *Silent Spring*. 40th anniversary ed. Boston, MA: Houghton Mifflin, 2002. 297.
5. Linda Lear. *Rachel Carson: Witness for Nature*. New York, NY: Henry Holt, 1997. 428.

Chapter 2. At the Top of Her Class

1. Linda Lear. *Rachel Carson: Witness for Nature*. New York, NY: Henry Holt, 1997. 13.
2. Linda Lear, ed. *Lost Woods: The Discovered Writing of Rachel Carson*. Boston, MA: Beacon Press, 1998. 148.
3. Linda Lear. *Rachel Carson: Witness for Nature*. New York, NY: Henry Holt, 1997. 22.
4. Linda Lear, ed. *Lost Woods: The Discovered Writing of Rachel Carson*. Boston, MA: Beacon Press, 1998. 13.
5. *Parnassus High School Yearbook*. Parnassus, PA: 1925.

Chapter 3. College and Graduate Student Days

1. Linda Lear. *Rachel Carson: Witness for Nature*. New York, NY: Henry Holt, 1997, 30.
2. Ibid. 132.
3. Margaret Fifer. "I remember Rachel." *Rachel Carson Collection*. 14 Aug. 2008 <www.chatham.edu/host/library/Carson/index.html>.
4. Linda Lear. *Rachel Carson: Witness for Nature*. New York, NY: Henry Holt, 1997, 60.
5. Linda Lear, ed. *Lost Woods: The Discovered Writings of Rachel Carson*. Boston, MA: Beacon Press, 1998. 148.
6. Rachel Carson. "Letter to Mary Frye." 8 Feb. 1930. *Rachel Carson History Project*. Rachel Carson Council, Inc., Chevy Chase, MD.

Chapter 4. Combining Science and Writing
1. Linda Lear, ed. *Lost Woods: The Discovered Writing of Rachel Carson*. Boston, MA: Beacon Press, 1998. 149.
2. Ibid.
3. Linda Lear. *Rachel Carson: Witness for Nature*. New York, NY: Henry Holt, 1997. 86–87.
4. Linda Lear, ed. *Lost Woods: The Discovered Writings of Rachel Carson*. Boston, MA: Beacon Press, 1998. 4.
5. Rachel Carson. *Under the Sea Wind: A Naturalist's Picture of Ocean Life*. New York, NY: Simon & Schuster, 1941. xiii.
6. Lisa H. Sideris and Kathleen Dean Moore, eds. *Rachel Carson: Legacy and Challenges*. New York, NY: SUNY Press, 2008. 155.

Chapter 5. Rising through the Ranks
1. Paul Brooks, ed. *The House of Life: Rachel Carson at Work*. 1972. Boston, MA: Houghton Mifflin, 1989. 72.
2. Linda Lear. *Rachel Carson: Witness for Nature*. New York, NY: Henry Holt, 1997. 133.
3. Linda Lear, ed. *Lost Woods: The Discovered Writing of Rachel Carson*. Boston, MA: Beacon Press, 1998. 231.
4. Mark H. Lytle. *The Gentle Subversive: Rachel Carson, Silent Spring, and the Rise of the Environmental Movement*. New York, NY: Oxford University Press, 2007. 62.
5. Rachel Carson. *The Sea Around Us*. New York, NY: Oxford University Press, 1979. 212.
6. Paul Brooks, ed. *The House of Life: Rachel Carson at Work*. 1972. Boston, MA: Houghton Mifflin, 1989. 123–124.
7. Ibid. 124.
8. Ibid.

Chapter 6. Best-selling Author
1. Jonathan Norton Leonard. "—And His Wonders in the Deep: A Scientist Draws an Intimate Portrait of the Winding Sea." *New York Times*. 1 July 1951. 4 Aug. 2008 <http://www.nytimes.com/books/97/10/05/reviews/carson-sea.html?_r=1&oref=slogin>.

SOURCE NOTES CONTINUED

2. Linda Lear. *Rachel Carson: Witness for Nature*. New York, NY: Henry Holt, 1997. 203.
3. Rachel Carson. "Letter to Dorothy Freeman." 23 Jan. 1962. *Always, Rachel: The Letters of Rachel Carson and Dorothy Freeman 1952–1964*. Ed. Martha Freeman. Boston, MA: Beacon Press, 1995. 394.
4. Linda Lear, ed. *Lost Woods: The Discovered Writings of Rachel Carson*. Boston, MA: Beacon Press, 1998. 80.
5. Rachel Carson. "Speech." National Symphony Orchestra luncheon and fundraiser, Mayflower Hotel, Washington DC. Rachel Carson Papers, Yale Collection of American Literature. 15 Sept. 1951.

Chapter 7. By the Edge of the Sea
1. Paul Brooks. *The House of Life: Rachel Carson at Work*. Boston, MA: Houghton Mifflin, 1972, 1989. 157.
2. Rachel Carson. *The Edge of the Sea*. Boston, MA: Houghton Mifflin, 1955. 1.
3. Mark H. Lytle. *The Gentle Subversive: Rachel Carson, Silent Spring, and the Rise of the Environmental Movement*. New York, NY: Oxford University Press, 2007. 109.

Chapter 8. Dreams and Realities
1. Linda Lear. *Rachel Carson: Witness for Nature*. New York, NY: Henry Holt, 1997. 298.
2. Rachel Carson. *The Sense of Wonder*. 1956. New York, NY: Harper & Row, 1998. 23.
3. Linda Lear. *Rachel Carson: Witness for Nature*. New York, NY: Henry Holt, 1997. 322.
4. Rachel Carson. "Letter to Dorothy Freeman." 1 Feb.1958. *Always, Rachel: The Letters of Rachel Carson and Dorothy Freeman 1952–1964*. Ed. Martha Freeman. Boston, MA: Beacon Press, 1995. 248–249.
5. Ibid. 248.

Chapter 9. Fighting the Battle

1. Rachel Carson. *Silent Spring*. 40th anniversary ed. Boston, MA: Houghton Mifflin, 2002. 12.
2. "Pesticides: The Price for Progress." *Time*. 28 Sept. 1962. 48.
3. Rachel Carson. *Silent Spring*. 40th anniversary ed. Boston, MA: Houghton Mifflin, 2002. 42.
4. Ibid. 135.
5. Ibid. 60.
6. William O. Douglas. *My Wilderness: The Pacific West*. New York, NY: Doubleday, 1960. N. pag.
7. Rachel Carson. *Silent Spring*. 40th anniversary ed. Boston, MA: Houghton Mifflin, 2002. 69.
8. Linda Lear. *Rachel Carson: Witness for Nature*. New York, NY: Henry Holt, 1997. 395.
9. Ibid.
10. Ibid.

Chapter 10. The Legacy of Rachel Carson

1. Public Law 88-577 (US Congress 1131-1136).
2. Edward O. Wilson. "On *Silent Spring*." *Courage for the Earth: Writers, Scientists, and Activists Celebrate the Life and Writing of Rachel Carson*. Ed. Peter Matthieson. Boston, MA: Houghton Mifflin, 2007. 36.
3. Margaret Mead. *Culture and Commitment: A Study of the Generation Gap*. New York, NY: Doubleday/Natural History Press, 1970.
4. Linda Lear. "Rachel Carson never called for DDT ban." 1 Sept. 2008 <http://www.earthsky.org/article/linda-lear_guest-post?>.
5. U.S. Congress, Senate Committee on Government Operations, 88th Cong., 1st session, June 4, 1963, 206.
6. Al Gore. "Rachel Carson and *Silent Spring*." *Courage for the Earth: Writers, Scientists, and Activists Celebrate the Life and Writing of Rachel Carson*. Ed. Peter Matthieson. Boston, MA: Houghton Mifflin, 2007. 67.

INDEX

ABOUT THE AUTHOR

Scott Gillam is a former English teacher and an editor of social studies and language arts textbooks. He is also the author of biographies of Steve Jobs and Andrew Carnegie in the *Essential Lives* series. He lives with his family in New York City.

PHOTO CREDITS

AP Images, cover, 76, 85; Loomis Dean/Time & Life Pictures/ Getty Images, 6, 11; CBS Photo Archive/Getty Images, 15; Rachel Carson Collection, College Archives, Chatham College, 16, 24, 33; Rachel Carson Council, Inc., 18, 23, 28, 44, 72, 75, 79; Underwood & Underwood/Corbis, 34; U.S. Fish and Wildlife Service, 38, 62; Heather Forcier/AP Images, 43; Bill Schaefer/ AP Images, 46; Hank Walker/Time & Life Pictures/Getty Images, 53; Alfred Eisenstaedt/Time & Life Pictures/Getty Images, 54, 61, 67, 68; Leonard McCombe/Time & Life Pictures/Getty Images, 56; John and Karen Hollingsworth/U.S. Fish and Wildlife Service, 86; Hal Korber/AP Images, 89; Shirley A. Briggs/Rachel Carson Council, Inc., 95